MW00623025

MINDFUL LIKE A CATHOLIC

A Catholic Approach to Mindful Living

Susan Brinkmann, OCDS

CATHOLIC LIFE INSTITUTE

PRESS

PO Box 1173
Pottstown, PA 19464
www.CatholicLifeInstitute.org

NIHIL OBSTAT:
Robert A. Pesarchick, STD, STL, MA, M.Div

IMPRIMATUR:
Archbishop Charles J. Chaput, OFM Cap.
No. 00018, July 8, 2019

Copyright © 2019 by Susan Brinkmann, OCDS

All rights reserved. No part of this publication may be reproduced, distributed or transmitted in any form or by any means, without prior written permission.

Catholic Life Institutes Press
PO Box 1173
Pottstown, PA 19464
www.CatholicLifeInstitute.org

Book Layout © 2021 Elizabeth Racine, www.ElizabethRacine.com

Cover Design by IGD Graphic Design, www.image-gd.com

Mindful Like a Catholic/ Susan Brinkmann, OCDS – 1st ed.
ISBN-13: 978-1-7336724-3-6

"The books the Holy Spirit is writing are living, and every soul a volume in which the divine author makes a true revelation of His word, explaining to every heart, unfolding it in every moment."

Father J. P. De Caussade

CONTENTS

You may be surprised to know that the two devotions you are about to discover have been around for hundreds of years. And yet just like so many treasures that are lost beneath the clutter of our lives, these gems remain as priceless as ever. They need only to be re-discovered, dusted off, and woven back into the fabric of our day.

In regard to the two devotions we are about to explore – the Sacrament of the Present Moment and the Practice of the Presence of God – this will certainly be a timely rediscovery. Being *mindful* is the hottest new psycho-spiritual trend of our day and many are clamoring to acquire its promised focus and subsequent release from the anxiety-inducing busyness of 21st century life. Many want to learn it, but not everyone wants to learn it the way it is being offered under the trendy term of *mindfulness.*

For starters, the version so popular today is derived from Buddhism and fits neatly into the category of "New Age thought control" with its emphasis on the desire to expand awareness of the Self. Essentially an eastern mental practice, its aim is to make you aware of the present moment in such a way that you just observe it without judging it to be one way or the other.

For instance, you're sitting here with a book in your hands, in your favorite chair, reading the words and feeling comfortable or tired or stiff or hungry – but none of that matters. It's just what *is*.

" ... [M]indfulness is what arises when you pay attention, on purpose, in the present moment, non-judgmentally, and as if your life depended on it."[1]

Psychologists say that this practice helps people to live in the now rather than in our minds, and use it to treat a variety of conditions from PTSD to depression and various anxiety disorders. But what they often neglect to tell their patients is that the way one learns to become mindful is by employing Buddhist meditation techniques.

As I explain in my book, *A Catholic Guide to Mindfulness*, the practice of mindfulness is derived from the Buddhist tradition and is the seventh step in the Noble Eightfold Path, which Buddhists believe is a process that leads to awakening to one's true nature. They call it Right-Mindfulness – which means controlling thoughts by maintaining awareness and focus on the present moment.

The way it's practiced usually involves some kind of meditation technique such as the following:

The person starts out by focusing on the sensation of sitting in the chair, on the feel of his feet on the floor, the position of his back and his head. He either closes his eyes or fixes his gaze on a spot about five feet in front of him and focuses intently on that spot.

He then asks himself, "What is my experience right now? What thoughts are present to me? What am I feeling?"

---

1 Kabat-Zinn, Jon, *Mindfulness for Beginners* (Boulder, Colorado: *Sounds True*, 2012) pg. 17

He then observes these thoughts and feelings without any need to judge them as good or bad, or to alter them in any way. They are just what *is*.

Next, the person attempts to let go of the contents of his mind by bringing his attention to his breath, such as how it is flowing out of his nostrils or in the rising and falling of his chest. By doing this, the person gives his mind only one thing to do.

In addition to the above example, which is known as Breathing Space Meditation, there are other Buddhist meditation techniques as well, such as Body Scan meditation where the person focuses on one part of the body at a time, starting with the feet and slowly moving up to the head.

This is probably a good place to pause and ask you, the reader an important question - does anything that I've been describing to you thus far sound like Christian meditation?

Of course not. Christian meditation is all about God, whereas Buddhist meditation – regardless of why it's being used – is all about the self. These two forms of meditation, with their diametrically opposed philosophies, just don't mesh no matter how much you try to manipulate them one way or the other.

This was a real problem for Jon Kabat-Zinn, the man who introduced the modern mindfulness fad to the largely Christian West. It was just *too* Buddhist.

A biomedical scientist and a practicing Buddhist, Kabat-Zinn always believed his karmic assignment was to find a way to bring his dharma practice together with his scientific pursuits to create one unified whole. While on a vipassana retreat, he had a vision in which he "saw" a way to do this, through a program he would later call the

Mindfulness Based Stress Reduction (MBSR) program. This program was designed to be a patient-centered approach which would employ the Buddhist practice of mindfulness in hospital settings to treat persons with PTSD and other stress/anxiety disorders.

However, with the core of the program being intensive training in mindfulness meditation, he knew these Buddhist roots would make many people nervous, so he "bent over backward"[2] to find ways to employ the program without revealing its Buddhist roots – a ploy that is still being used today.

As Zinn admitted, the instructions he gave to those who will teach MBSR is that it would be "hugely helpful" if they have a strong personal grounding in the Buddadharma and its teachings; however, at the same time, he instructed them to be careful to bring only the essence of these Buddhist roots into the classroom.

This subterfuge continued as the practice made its way into mainstream medicine and mental health care, and from there into the boardroom and even the classroom where it inevitably began to infringe on people's religious liberty. For this reason, attorneys at the American Center for Law and Justice are currently in the process of suing, at both the state and federal levels, to have the practice of mindfulness removed from schools because it imposes an unconstitutional religious influence in state-funded schools.

Although Zinn and many other health care professionals try to get around this argument by insisting that mindfulness is non-spiritual and can be detached from its Buddhist roots, many the experts wholeheartedly disagree.

---

2 Kabat-Zinn, Jon, Ph.D., "Some Reflections on the Origins of MBSR," *Contemporary Buddhism, Vol. 12, No. 1,* May 2011

"Though mindfulness is often learned or practiced in a secular manner, individuals often report spiritual benefits from their practice. On the whole, research suggests that mindfulness and spirituality are overlapping but distinct constructs, that they likely interact and contribute to one another's development, and that both are important mechanisms through which MBIs [mindfulness-based interventions] exert benefits."[3]

In fact, when Kabat-Zinn was confronted with the question of whether or not mindfulness was a "spiritual" practice during a panel discussion, he chose to evade the answer: "Well, that depends on what you mean by spiritual," he remarked.[4]

When asked if it could be "secularized," as many psychologists claim it can be, Kabat-Zinn again dismissed the idea.

"I assiduously avoid the word secular," he said. "As soon as you say secular mindfulness, you're abstracting the sacred out of it."[5]

As a result, many Christians - who are not being fully informed that the methods used to teach them how to be mindful originate in a non-Christian religion - are becoming involved in Eastern meditation techniques.

Some are taking it further than just using it to calm their anxiety. Many Christians are deciding that the calming effects of Buddhist meditation are a great way to improve

---

3 Kim-Preito, Chu, *Religion and Spirituality Across Cultures,* (New York, NY: *Springer,* 2014) quoting Chapter 11, "Mindfulness, Consciousness, Spirituality, and Well-Being" by Emily L. B. Lykons, pg. 203
4 Nour Foundation, "Is Mindfulness a Spiritual Practice?" February 19, 2013, accessed on YouTube.
5 Baer, Drake, "The Father of Mindfulness on What Mindfulness Has Become," *Thrive Global*, April 12, 2017.

their focus in prayer and are thus including these practices in their prayer life, to their detriment.

Combining two types of prayer that originate in incompatible religious philosophies doesn't work. This is particularly true for those whose spiritual life has not yet matured enough to understand that the Christian seeks prayer to improve his or her relationship with God, not because it is "calming" and "relaxing" and full of "enlightenment." These motives for prayer make one susceptible to the seduction of eastern meditation techniques which are designed to produce the kind of altered state that naturally appeals to the senses. Many a well-intentioned Catholic has been diverted into eastern mysticism simply because they were not well-schooled in the ways of the interior life and succumbed to the lure of the "feel good" spiritual experiences found in the east.

For example, several years ago, a distraught wife and mother sent an email to me about her husband who had taken up a twice-daily practice of mindfulness and body scan meditation for stress. One day, he decided to skip family prayer to practice mindfulness meditation instead. When she confronted him about it, saying that prayer is more restful, he disagreed and said this was not his experience, and to leave him alone.

What her husband didn't realize until it was too late is that Buddhist meditation techniques and Catholic prayer move in two different directions. One leads to God, the other leads to the Self. As, a result, this man eventually abandoned Catholic prayer altogether in exchange for the "quick fix" of Eastern meditation.

The spiritual risks are only part of the dangers lurking behind the hype of today's mindfulness craze. In spite of the headlines touting study after study alleging the efficacy of this practice, serious research has found that the vast majority of studies conducted on mindfulness are not scientifically sound.

For example, in 2014, researchers at Johns Hopkins University in Baltimore, Maryland reviewed nearly 19,000 meditation studies and came up with only 47 that met their criteria for a well-designed study. And of those 47 studies, results indicated only a small to moderate effect of mindfulness in reducing emotional symptoms and no evidence that mindfulness programs were better than other treatments.

This lack of evidence in support of a practice that has now made its way from hospitals and therapy couches to the board room and even elementary schools, caused 15 prominent scientists to publish an article in 2017 in a prestigious scientific journal calling for more rigor and less hype in the burgeoning mindfulness industry.

"Misinformation and poor methodology associated with past studies of mindfulness may lead public consumers to be harmed, misled and disappointed," they wrote.[6]

The risks of investing one's mental health to this practice is not minimal. Credible research has uncovered a host of problems associated with mindfulness and eastern meditation such as depersonalization, which is the feeling of being detached from your mental processes or body, and psychosis, which is the loss of contact with reality accompanied by delusions. Other problems include hallucinations, disorganized speech, feelings of anxiety, increased risk of seizures, loss of appetite, and insomnia.

---

6 Van Dam, Nicholas T., et al, "Mind the Hype: A Critical Evaluation and Prescriptive Agenda for Research on Mindfulness and Meditation," *Perspectives on Psychological Science*, October 10, 2017.

How common are these problems? A study conducted at the University of California in Irvine found that 63 percent of the group studied had suffered at least one negative effect.

We shouldn't be surprised by this because mindfulness, in spite of its endorsement by mental health practitioners, is just another kind of New Age "thought control" program – all of which are based on flimsy science. In fact, according to the American Psychological Association, 95 percent of the books in the self-help aisle at Barnes & Noble have no clinical evidence to prove their claims.[7] These include the works of best-selling gurus like Deepak Chopra, Tony Robbins, Marianne Williamson, and the late Dr. Wayne Dyer. They are very much in the business of selling this "new" kind of thought control, such as *The Secret* and *The Law of Attraction*, which teach a person that if they use their mind correctly, they can attract good fortune and well-being.

All of these practices give a power to the mind that it really doesn't have – and in doing so, they make the mind into a kind of god.

Mindfulness is just the latest edition, but the quest to control the mind isn't new, nor is it necessarily a bad thing depending on how you go about it.

Even Christians suffer from destructive thought patterns to some extent or another, so we could all use some help in this area. This help needn't come in the form of New Age and/or other non-Christian methods because we have our own methods for thought control, and they come straight from Scripture.

---

7 American Psychological Association, accessed online at https://www.apa.org/monitor/jan08/recommended

St. Paul says to the Philippians: " ... [W]hatever is true, whatever is honorable, whatever is just, whatever is pure, whatever is lovely, whatever is gracious, if there is any excellence and if there is anything worthy of praise, think about these things... Then the God of peace will be with you."[8]

This is Christian thought control and the type we will soon be learning how to put into effect so that we can live in the present moment, in the presence of our God, not for the sake of our Self, but for the sake of being with the One Who created these minds of ours and knows exactly how they work. While this devotional method is not intended to replace recommended treatment for mental health conditions, it's the perfect complement for those who simply want to "live mindfully" - but without the Buddhist trappings.

After plumbing the depths of these treasures, the Christian will quickly learn that our method of thought control is far more effective than the Buddhist variety. Even those psychologists who try to "Catholicize" mindfulness by employing Buddhist meditation methods sandwiched between Catholic devotional practices are doomed to failure when it comes to helping someone lead a more mindful life. While these methods may work for a while, if the underlying state of the soul is not correctly prepared, no psychological method can offer a lasting effect.

First, because only God, not ourselves and the alleged power of our minds, has the capability to heal us of whatever is causing the negative thoughts or other anxiety-causing ruminations of the mind.

Second, because the mind is a well-known spiritual battleground, and the inability to focus is just one of many ploys used by Satan to oppress the faithful, Jesus Christ is

---

8 Phil. 4:8-9

our only means to uncover and then defeat this diabolical deception.

Third, because Jesus Himself calls us to exercise this kind of control, we can count on His grace to enable us to do so. This is far better than having to rely on our own weak and often inconsistent efforts as would be the case when practicing today's popular Buddhist-based mindfulness.

By the time you finish this book, you will understand why there is no comparison between the two Catholic practices we are about to explore and Jon Kabat-Zinn's karmic assignment of blending science and Buddhism.

Compared to the broad reach of the practice of the presence of God and the sacrament of the present moment, mindfulness is nothing more than what it is - a sterile mental exercise that focuses on a single dimension of life – that which concerns only the self. There is no reciprocal awareness or loving or sharing with Another - our God. It is empty of all but ourselves.

In fact, allow me to go so far as to say that the Christian equivalent of mindfulness, which is living in the present moment in the presence of God, not only replaces mindfulness, it far surpasses it.

Where mindfulness offers a momentary escape from anxiety, the Christian alternative offers a *solution* to anxiety.

Instead of being aimed at a momentary improvement, the Christian version offers permanent transformation.

One is a quick fix, the other is a long-term opportunity for exponential personal growth toward the ultimate goal of our existence here on earth – union with God.

By the time we reach this summit of union with Him here on earth, we will have been freed from the source of all the misery and anxiety in our lives – sin.

We will have been completely transformed into a totally new creation – not just an improvement of the old – but someone entirely new.

When we are united with our Creator who exists in the present moment, we will finally become who we were meant to be from the beginning of time – which is a grace that surpasses all understanding.

CHAPTER ONE

THE SACRAMENT
OF THE
PRESENT MOMENT

"God speaks to every individual through what happens to them moment by moment."[9]

In this simple sentence, Father J.P. de Caussade, SJ, one of the greatest spiritual directors in the history of the Church, sums up the essence of the practice that has come to be known as the "sacrament of the present moment."

On this path, we learn that Christ comes to us in a unique and personal way every day, and in every moment of every day. For this reason, our attention must remain focused on all of the events that occur, minute-by-minute, from the trivial to the sublime, because this is how God speaks to us. All of the moments of our day and the simple duties that make up those moments, achieve sacramental significance. All moments are important, regardless of how insignificant they might seem.

---

9 De Caussade, Jean-Pierre, *The Sacrament of the Present Moment*, translated by Kitty Muggeridge (New York NY; *HarperCollins Publishers*, 1989) pg. xiii

"No moment is trivial," he writes, "since each one contains a divine Kingdom, and heavenly sustenance."[10]

It is only when one fully comprehends such a sublime truth that we can sing: "Precious moment, how small in the eyes of my head and how great in those of my heart, the means whereby I receive small things from the Father who reigns in heaven! Everything that falls from there is very excellent, everything bears the mark of its maker."[11]

Think about it! The making of a pot of coffee, scrubbing dishes, driving to the bank, standing in line at the supermarket, taking off your shoes, brushing your teeth – in all of it we find the touch of Our Creator along with His will for that particular moment in our life, regardless of how mundane it may seem.

Unlike the Buddhist equivalent of mindfulness, which would call upon us to focus on these trivial activities just for the sake of the activity, the Christian version seeks a much deeper revelation about both God and one self in the seemingly insignificant moments of life.

"The books the Holy Spirit is writing are living, and every soul a volume in which the divine author makes a true revelation of His word, explaining to every heart, unfolding it in every moment."[12]

The person of faith, who is focused on each moment of life, is in a constant state of learning and discovery.

"The present holds infinite riches beyond your wildest dreams but you will only enjoy them to the extent of

---

10 Ibid, xix
11 Ibid
12 Ibid, pg. 74

your faith and love. The more a soul loves, the more it longs, the more it hopes, the more it finds."[13]

The question then becomes a simple one – on what is our attention primarily focused throughout the day? On what we're doing at the moment, on what we wish we were doing, on what we will be doing later, or on what we did yesterday? If this were a multiple choice question, most of us would probably choose, "all of the above." Even while engrossed in our daily duties, the mind likes to wander off, which means even the most focused among us can fall short when it comes to staying present.

This is especially true in those moments of our life when we're alone, either unoccupied, or doing something mundane. It is in these moments that resisting the urge to daydream and remaining focused on the moment seem, well, almost impossible. Who wants to focus on mopping the floor or pulling weeds in the garden?

Believe it or not, spiritual masters tell us that if we want to know what's going on inside of ourselves, paying close attention to the thoughts that occupy our minds during these seemingly inconsequential moments of life are of upmost importance.

This is particularly true for those who are in search of their predominant fault, the defect in us that tends to prevail over all others and has the most negative influence on our behavior and temperament.

Toward what do my most ordinary preoccupations tend, in the morning when I awake, or when I am alone? Where do my thoughts and desires go spontaneously?

When we live in the present, we will find these goldmines of personal information hiding in the moment

---

13 Ibid, pg. 62

simply because this is where God is and He can choose to reveal Himself – or our self – anytime He wants.

Perhaps this is why so many of us would rather not pay attention to the present. Leaping into the future, reminiscing about the past can be, for some, an escape from having to face the hard realities that can only be viewed in the present tense.

Is it any wonder that the brutal simplicity of the "present moment" is where saints are formed? Whether we realize it or not, staying in the here and now, focused on whatever God may be revealing to us, is the most direct route to sanctity. Because it is here that we confront who we are, where we're going, what we want – and don't want.

As ironic as it might seem, the answers to these profound questions about ourselves are usually answered in the moments of life that we pay the least attention to.

Why?

"Because it is there that who we truly are comes to the surface," explains Kitty Muggeridge, De Caussade's translator. "In the big events – when we are on public display – we can hide what is inside fairly well, and even in the intimacy of our families we can put on a good front for some time; but in the unguarded moment, the true self will surface. And once we can face, before God, who we truly are, we have stepped onto the path of grace that leads to conformity to the image of Christ."[14]

The Christian focus on the present is not about an escape into a meaningless moment of pause as it would be in the Buddhist version, but a direct challenge to face what God might be showing us about ourselves – and our relation to Him - in that moment.

---

14 Ibid, xx

"The courage to face the inner monsters takes a faith and trust in God that many of us do not possess (or don't want to possess), and so we busy ourselves with muchness and manyness and undertake our colossal enterprises to avoid looking inside."[15]

This is when the thoughts come crashing in on us that reveal who we truly are inside – while sitting in stalled traffic, picking up after the family for the umpteenth time that day, sitting through the mind-numbing monotony of seeing the same TV commercial yet again.

It's easy to see why this brilliantly uncomplicated path is one that makes itself available to everyone regardless of their education, rank, or financial status. A farmer sowing wheat in a field is as likely to achieve the heights of holiness on this path as is a theologian with degrees from the Pontifical universities.

Even more remarkable, it has been this way since the days of our forefathers, those giants of the faith who did not have access to any of the spiritual direction, hagiography, or volumes of theology that are available to us today.

"The spiritual life was then a matter of immediate communication with God. . . . All they knew was that each moment brought its appointed task, faithfully to be accomplished," de Caussade writes. "This was enough for the spiritually-minded of those days. All their attention was focused on the present, minute by minute; like the hand of a clock that marks the minutes of each hour covering the distance along which it has to travel. Constantly prompted by divine impulsion, they found themselves imperceptibly turned toward the next task that God had ready for them at each hour of the day."[16]

---

15 *Ibid*
16 Ibid, pg. 1

Our Blessed Lady gives us the perfect example of what it means to live in the present moment when she told the angel, "Be it unto me according to thy word,"[17] a response which, according to De Caussade, summed up the whole mystical teaching of her ancestors.

"Everything was reduced, as it is now, to the purest and simplest commitment to the will of God in what ever form it might present itself."[18]

In the case of Our Blessed Lady, this divine will ruled her life. And she discovered that will, not only in the great events of her life – the Annunciation, the Nativity, the Presentation, the Crucifixion – but in every nook and cranny of her existence in Nazareth.

"Whether her occupations were exalted or lowly, in her eyes they were but shadows, more or less luminous, in which she found it possible both to worship God and to recognize the works of the Almighty."[19]

By doing so, she looked upon everything that she was called to do in the course of a day, whether it be a joy or a sorrow, as a gift from God, and was thus "nourished neither by the world nor by fantasy, but by Him alone."[20]

Imagine what it would be like to live life in such a simple and yet profound way! We would find nourishment for our souls in everything, from that first sip of coffee in the morning to the traffic jam on our way to work to the physical exertion of an evening jog – all things we would otherwise overlook, pass off as a useless annoyance or a necessary pain. By ignoring these moments, we miss how

---

17 Luke 1:38
18 *The Sacrament of the Present Moment*, p. 2
19 Ibid
20 Ibid

delicious is that first sip of coffee, how sitting in bumper-to-bumper traffic can be the perfect time to be alone with God, how cool and refreshing is the wind on our face as we struggle to run uphill.

For example, let us take this very moment as our first practice in experiencing life in the present. If you are reading this book in the present moment according to the popular Buddhist method, you would be expected to notice such things as how the chair feels beneath you, how the book feels in your hand, how smooth the paper is as you turn the pages. Whatever thoughts come into your mind as a result of what you're reading are not to be judged one way or the other – they are whatever they are.

Now let's try the same exercise in the Christian way. As you sit in the chair, holding this book in your hands, you realize that God gave you this opportunity, that He probably put into your heart whatever longings made you reach for this particular volume. Notice what this says to you about the tender way God is loving you in this moment, how He responds to the movements of your heart and chooses to feed you with precisely what you were hungering for. Gratitude naturally wells up in your heart and this feeling, along with the knowledge that what you are doing is in conformity with God's will, enhances everything that you are reading, thinking, feeling, as you read this book.

In both examples, our eyes are opened to the hidden nuances about the moment that might have otherwise gone unnoticed, but it's plain to see how much more profound is the experience of the Christian method. Being present – with our Great and Mighty God – in the moment, makes all the difference in the world. What one might see as a nuance of the moment in the Buddhist method, becomes a gift to be treasured by the Christian.

In addition, by remaining focused on the present moment and seeing each moment as a gift from God, we learn so much about Him in the choices He makes for us, how benevolent and yet balanced He is in how He manages our lives – giving us just enough joy and sorrow to form us into strong and capable servants.

And through it all we watch ourselves grow, step by step, moment by moment, ever so gradually becoming stronger in faith, more resilient in hope, and more deliberate in charity.

Some fear that in order to let God act in everything while we focus only on love and obedience to the present moment means that we must remain passive and inactive, but this is hardly the case. In fact, it's the exact opposite. We are not to behave like inert beings who sit around with their eyes cast heavenward, waiting for the next moment to arrive.

Instead, the Christian is called to be "active in everything needed for the fulfilment of their duty to the present moment, but passive and submissive and self-forgetting in everything else; only meekly waiting on the divine will. . . One loves God, one does one's Christian duty, frequents the sacraments, observes the external religious practices that are required of everyone. One obeys superiors, civil duties are performed, impulses of the flesh, the blood and the devil are continually resisted. or no one is more scrupulous in acquitting themselves of all these obligations than those set on this course."[21]

Others believe that living this way means we don't plan for the future and recklessly leave everything for God to handle.

---

21 *Sacrament of the Present Moment*, pg. 11

Not so!

"We are obliged to plan for the future and take thought for tomorrow," advises Father Jacque Philippe. "But we should do it *without worrying*, without the care that gnaws at the heart but doesn't solve anything – and often prevents us from putting our hearts into what we have to do here and now."[22]

You may be thinking, "this sounds too difficult! Surely only the saints are capable of living this way, not ordinary people like me!"

This is only true if one believes saints can only be people like Thomas Aquinas or Catherine of Siena.

As De Caussade warns, we must beware of this temptation because God makes His saints as He pleases.

"[T]o imagine that . . . souls are more or less perfect merely because their duties are more exalted, is to place perfection, not in surrender to God's will, but in the duties themselves."[23]

On the other hand, we must not make light of the effort needed to live this way. To be this mindful of the present moment *is* hard – whether you're doing it the Buddhist way or the Christian way; however, as we learned in the last chapter, the Christian has a distinct advantage. We have the grace of God to help us. Those who attempt this via the Buddhist route are on their own. It's not hard to deduce who has the better chance for success.

Perhaps the first and most important step in learning how to live this way is to acquire a desire to do so.

---

22 Philippe, Father Jacques, *Interior Freedom* (New York, NY; *Scepter,* 2007) pg. 87
23 *Sacrament of the Present Moment,* pg. 58

"As soon as their heart is willing, souls come under the influence of divine action, whose power over them depends on the extent to which they have surrendered themselves. Love is the way to this surrender,"[24]de Caussade writes.

Let this be the first grace we ask for – the desire to live in the present moment. If we don't have that desire right now, if we're a bit fearful and not yet ready to commit ourselves, then ask Him for the grace to desire it.

Rest assured, Our Lord wants only to help us with this because He created us to be happy and contented in this life. We were designed for happiness, not to be running around at a frantic pace, perpetually time-starved, and forever anxious about tomorrow.

As Father Reginald Garrigou-Lagrange explains, "the desire for happiness is not a mere hypothetical wish; it is innate, with its immediate foundation in nature itself."[25]

The reason we're not happy is because we have a bad habit of looking for happiness in all the wrong places. The innate desire for happiness that Father Lagrange speaks about is not the superficial kind. It's not based upon mere pleasurable sensations that are found in possessions or high honors. Neither can it be found in eastern meditation techniques that offer us a brief escape from our troubles by stripping our minds of all thoughts and leaving us in an empty void; nor can it be found in the call to become hyper-focused on how our bodies are feeling in the present moment. Even while pursuing these things with the greatest energy, deep down inside we still know that something is missing.

This inner knowledge springs from our innate desire for real happiness, the kind we were designed to enjoy. This

---

24 Ibid pg. 32
25 Garrigou-Lagrange, Fr. Reginald, OP, *Providence* (Rockford, IL; *Tan Books and Publishers, Inc.*, 1937), pg. 45

is a deeper and more lasting joy, the kind that can only be found at the point where we reach the summit of our existence which is where we discover the purpose for our creation. It is a summit that can only be found in the heart of the One who created us.

Whether we realize it or not, our soul naturally desires to live forever with the One who created it and we will have no peace until we rest in Him.

For this reason, the happiest and most satisfied life is that which is lived closest to Him - which is precisely what the sacrament of the present moment, and its companion devotion, the practice of the presence of God, is designed to do.

Practicum

1. Is there anything about living in the present moment that makes you feel uncomfortable? Perhaps you are unhappy with where your life is right now and don't want to look at it that closely. Maybe the thought of spending less time dwelling on future plans gives you a feeling of insecurity. Whatever it is, jot it down here and give it to God to deal with as He wills.

_____

_____

_____

_____

_____

_____

_____

_____

_____

2. Begin to pray daily for God's help in learning how to "slow down and smell the roses" that He sends into your life – even the ones with thorns! For example, *"Lord, I want to see you in every moment of my day, but I'm so busy running from this task to the next that I hardly notice you're even here. Help me to slow down, to focus on the now where I can find you waiting for me, longing to share every minute of life with me. Give me the desire to open up my life to you, from the big moments to the most mundane, and the wisdom to see your hand in all."* Make up your own prayer here:

_____

_____

_____

_____

_____

_____

_____

_____

_____

3. For five minutes every day (use the stopwatch on your smartphone or some other means to time yourself until you get the hang of it), practice living in the present moment by using your senses to observe everything you can about that moment – everything that you are feeling, seeing, hearing, tasting. For example, notice how the sun is shining or the sound of the rain on the roof, the hum of the car's engine as you drive down the road or the feel of the sidewalk under your feet, the people you are encountering or the stillness of the house, the taste of the food you are enjoying or the hunger in your stomach. Realize that

each of these observations is a communication from God Who meant it exclusively for you. What is He saying to you? What would you like to say to Him in response? What has this observation told you about God? What has it told you about yourself? At the end of the five minutes, jot down everything you discovered as well as all that you might have missed about these moments if you had not been paying such close attention. Record some of these observations here:

_____

_____

_____

_____

_____

_____

_____

_____

_____

_____

4. Practice this five-minute exercise at different times during the day so that you can experience a good cross-section of your daily life. For example, upon waking in the morning, while occupied with your daily duties, and relaxing after dinner.

CHAPTER TWO

PEACE OF MIND,
PEACE OF SOUL

When we remain in the present moment, which naturally keeps us close to God who exists in the present, we can't help but experience a kind of supernatural joy that somehow manages to remain steadfast and robust in spite of the upsets and trials of life.

This joy is called peace of soul and it is imperative for those who wish to acquire the kind of mindfulness that Jesus Himself recommended for His followers:

"So do not worry about tomorrow, for tomorrow will bring worries of its own. Today's trouble is enough for today."[26]

Fulton Sheen, who referred to the present moment as "the Now," offered the following reflection on this verse:

"This means that each day has its own trials; we are not to borrow troubles from tomorrow, because that day too will have its cross. We are to leave the past to divine mercy and to trust the future, whatever its trials, to God's loving providence. Each minute of life has its peculiar duty — regardless of the appearance that minute may take. The

26 Matthew 6:34

Now-moment is the moment of salvation. Each complaint against it is a defeat; each act of resignation to it is a victory."[27]

A victory indeed! Unlike God, who exists in eternity beyond the grips of time, we are prisoners of time and all of our anxieties relate to time.

For example, as Father Andrew Apostoli explains, "The past exerts an influence on us through our memory. We recall all kinds of events and experiences that we have had. The difficulty arises when our memory recalls only negative experiences such as hurts, injustices and gripes. As the saying goes, 'We are replaying the old tapes!' We keep reliving these negative experiences over and over again. The terrible feelings they provoke create a resentment in our hearts that we can end up taking to the grave. In the final analysis, the past has made even the present miserable."[28]

The future is equally distressing, especially when we allow our imaginations to run wild.

"Fears and worries, which are not actual but only potential, flood our minds and hearts with the most dire anxieties. These imaginations, which have not yet occurred and probably will never occur, affect us as if they were imminent and unavoidable. How much time and how much energy is lost in our lives because we let dread of the future grip us with a paralyzing fear that keeps us from doing anything with our lives?"[29]

---

27 Sheen, Archbishop Fulton, *From the Angel's Blackboard*, quoted by Father Andrew Apostoli in, "Living the Present Moment: The Wisdom of Archbishop Fulton Sheen," *Catholic Exchange*, accessed online.
28 *From the Angels Blackboard*
29 Ibid

Nothing is more useless – and more destructive to our inner peace – than worry about the future.

As de Caussade chides: "You may say, what will become of me in that case? Such a question is one more temptation from the devil. Why are we so skillful in tormenting ourselves beforehand with what will possibly never happen? Sufficient for the day be the evil thereof! Anxious forethought does us much harm; why do we indulge in it so readily? We are the enemies of our own peace of soul."[30]

Even worse, while we allow ourselves to be worried sick about the future, we aren't living in the present moment which means we are cutting ourselves off from the graces that are *only* available to us in that moment. Wherever God is, there is His grace; because God exists in the present moment, His graces can *only* be found in the present moment, not in the past or in the future.

"Hearts anxious about tomorrow can't be open to the grace of the present moment,"[31] writes Father Jacques Philippe.

So if the thought of a future event fills us with dread and fear, this is because the graces that would make us feel stronger and more capable of dealing with the event, aren't yet available to us. When we get there, God will give us the grace to handle it – but not before!

"Like the manna that fed the Hebrew people in the desert, grace can't be stockpiled. We can't build up reserves of grace but only receive it moment by moment as part of the 'daily bread' we pray for in the Our Father."[32]

Instead, we should accept the fact that things rarely happen as we expect and all of our worry is for naught.

---

30 *Self-Abandonment to Divine Providence*, pg. 324-325
31 *Interior Freedom,* pg. 88
32 Ibid

"Most of our fears and apprehensions turn out to be completely imaginary . . . It's better to accept things as they come, one after another, trusting that we will have the grace to deal with them at the right time, than to invent a host of scenarios about what may happen – scenarios that normally turn out to be wrong. The best way to prepare for the future is to put our hearts into the present."[33]

Anxious forethought is good for nothing but stirring up interior agitation that slowly deprives the soul of the ability to listen to and obey the voice of the Holy Spirit.

This inner turmoil can come in many forms; anxieties, vain fears, dejection, weariness, discouragement, all of which are either embraced or are at least not sufficiently resisted. Over time, this can wear us down until it finally wears us out.

"A sick and agitated mind is in the same case as a fever-weakened body that can perform no serious work until healed of its complaint."[34]

If we are to restore our peace of soul, and thereby remain in the present, we must quiet our mind by learning how to take control of our thoughts and stop allowing our mind to ruin our lives with its propensity toward constant ruminations, overthinking, letting our imaginations run wild.

As St. Paul teaches, we must put on "the mind of Christ."[35]

In order to do this, we must "take captive every thought to make it obedient to Christ."[36]

So how do we do that?

---

33 *Interior Freedom,* pg. 88
34 *Self-Abandonment to Divine Providence,* pg. 203
35 1 Cor 2:16
36 2 Cor 10:5

In his booklet, *Thought Control: Architect of Character*, Fr. John H. Hampsch, CMF says that we "take captive every thought" by remaining vigilant over what we allow into our minds in the first place.

"Erroneous input into a computer results in erroneous output. So it is with our minds. If we fill them with the garbage of sleazy literature or questionable television programs or films, with worldly conversation or thoughts of envy, jealousy, avarice, pride, morbid fear, resentment, etc. then we leave little or no room for God to work in us."[37]

Our minds must be changed! This is why we must do as St. Paul advises and, "put off your old self, which is being corrupted by its deceitful desires; be made new in the attitude of your minds ..."[38]

In order to accomplish this, however, we must remember that God has the power to change even the most destructive thought patterns.

"Thought patterns that have troubled you for years can be transformed by God's power, beginning right at this moment. If you allow that to happen your very life-style will change accordingly and you will enjoy a great sense of liberation for 'if the Son sets you free, you will be free indeed (John 8:36)'."[39]

We start this process by learning how to take seriously the Christian version of thought control that we learned about earlier in this course:

" ... [W]hatever is true, whatever is honorable, whatever is just, whatever is pure, whatever is lovely,

---

37 Hampsch, Father John F. CMF, *Thought Control: Architect of Character* (Santa Barbara, CA; Queenship Publishing Company) pg. 14
38 Ephesians 4:22-23
39 *Thought Control*, pg. 8

whatever is gracious, if there is any excellence and if there is anything worthy of praise, think about these things. ... Then the God of peace will be with you."[40]

For the Christian, it's easy to dwell upon *whatever is true* because we have the Word of God and know that Scripture is reliable.

"Inevitably, prayerful thinking about sublime truths will spawn high-minded habits. 'As a man thinks in his heart, so is he' (Prov. 23:7)."[41]

Whatever is noble are those thoughts that transcend pettiness, which is the cause of so many fights and quarrels.

"Noble thoughts are the parents of peace. This insight, if lived out, would be enough to empty our divorce courts."[42]

The person who wants to stay near to God naturally wants to think about *whatever is right* because "to do only what is right, one must be continually conscious of what is right" and will be careful to "put aside the deeds of darkness and behave decently (Romans 13:11-13)."[43]

Pondering upon *whatever is pure* keeps us within the realm of the kind of wisdom that comes from heaven, which is "first of all pure" (James 3:17).

"Thinking only pure thoughts makes one 'pure in heart,' a mentality to which Jesus attached a beatitudinal promise that 'they will see God' (Matt. 5:8)."[44]

---

40 Phil. 4:8-9
41 *Thought Control*, pg. 10
42 Ibid
43 Ibid, pg. 11
44 Ibid

The heart, in Biblical language, is the center of the human spirit from which springs all of our emotions, thoughts, motivations and actions. This means every attempt to discipline the mind in order to keep it pure is well worth the effort! As we read in Proverbs, "Above all, guard your heart, for it is the wellspring of life."[45]

Who does not want to dwell upon *whatever is lovely?* Instead of seeing the bad in our neighbor, dwell on whatever is lovely in them. "Chaste thoughts of such fascinating qualities of a person will eclipse their weak points and failings, thus making charity much easier to practice."[46]

When we ponder upon *whatever is amiable, whatever is gracious, whatever is excellent, whatever is praiseworthy*, we keep our minds filled with positive rather than negative thoughts.

This does not mean that we ignore the evil and the distasteful in our world. It simply means that we do not dwell upon what is evil and distasteful.

As we all know, the mind is the devil's playground. A thousand times a day he introduces sad, discouraging, anxious, fearful, and hateful thoughts into our minds and too many of us offer not a peep of resistance. Instead, we choose to sit and stew in our dark thoughts, rehashing that argument with a friend over and over in our minds, or conjuring up all kinds of reasons why we need to be suspicious or envious of our neighbor.

"Thoughts are enormously powerful, more than we usually realize," Father Hampsch says.[47]

---

45 Proverbs 4:23
46 *Thought Control*, pg. 12
47 Ibid

Remember, Cain harbored jealous thoughts and committed the first murder. Samson's lustful thoughts caused an entire nation to suffer and Haman's obsession with killing Mordecai led to his own death.

"Rogue thoughts are loose cannons on the deck," he explains. "Judas had a rogue thought – betraying Christ for a handful of silver – and his name became immortalized in infamy."[48]

When these thoughts come into our minds, we must rely on the power of God to help us regain control.

As de Caussade advises: " . . . [T]ake care never to harbor voluntarily in your heart any thought calculated to grieve, disquiet, or dishearten it. From one point of view, such thoughts are more dangerous than impure temptations. Your need then, is to allow them to pass you by, despising them and letting them fall like a stone into the sea. You must resist them by concentrating your attention upon contrary reflections."[49]

However, it's important to note that this resistance must be gentle!

" . . .[W]hile we are to put energy and generosity into our struggle, mildness, tranquility and peace are as necessary. For unquiet grieving and vexatious restlessness will make the remedy worse than the disease."[50]

It's also important to realize that the deep tranquility of soul that comes from living in the present moment is only acquired by degrees. It doesn't happen all at once.

---

48 Ibid
49 *Self-Abandonment to Divine Providence*, pg. 204
50 Ibid

"It is necessary, however, to undergo much toil before we can acquire this serenity, for our inexperience inevitably exposes us to the assaults of powerful enemies. But once acquired, this peace will bring untold consolation to our souls in their fight against the disquieting elements of the world, and daily we shall perfect the art of quieting the turmoil of the spirit."[51]

In those moments when we are enduring such calamity and commotion that we can barely think, let alone calm ourselves, our first recourse *must* be to pray. Even if it's just a short exclamation, "Jesus! Help!" or the recitation of a favorite verse, "The Lord is my shepherd, I shall not fear" (Psalm 23:1), prayer is essential to restoring our peace.

"Let us not be disturbed by the endless and pointless hurry of the business world; when we are at work, let us attend to business affairs with composure and ease, refraining from rigid conformity to a harsh, exacting schedule, and too great an eagerness to see our work done."[52]

We must also resist the temptation to become angry at ourselves for being troubled or upset and instead adopt the counsel of St. Frances de Sales who taught: "Neither be troubled that you are troubled, nor be anxious that you are anxious, nor be disturbed that you are disturbed, but turn naturally to God in sweet and peaceful humility, going so far as to thank Him that He has not allowed you to commit still greater faults."[53]

When we live in the present, casting anxious looks neither backward nor forward, we find peace of soul, and in that peace, we find the heart of God.

---

51 Scupoli, Dom Lorenzo, *The Spiritual Combat and a Treatise on Peace of Soul* (Rockford, IL; Tan Books and Publishers, 1945) pg. 199
52 *The Spiritual Combat*, page 200
53 Ibid, pg. 238

Practicum

1. It's time to take an inventory of our thoughts. On a scale of 1 to 10, with 10 being "all the time" and 1 being "hardly ever," how often do the following thoughts occupy your mind?

   _____ fearful

   _____ anxious/worried

   _____ critical (of self or others)

   _____ happy/positive

   _____ angry

   _____ sad

2. Prayerfully read Philippians 4:8-9 and give yourself a grade of A-F on how well your thoughts conform to the biblical standard. _____

3. Now that you have an idea of what kind of thoughts are occupying – or not occupying – your mind all day, prayerfully work with the Holy Spirit to discern what might be at the root of your destructive thought patterns, whether it is relationship troubles or conflicts in the office or in other areas of your life. Write them down here and bring them to Jesus for healing and ask Him to restore your peace of mind.

   _____

   _____

   _____

   _____

   _____

   _____

   _____

4. While continuing to work through these areas in your daily prayer, develop a plan to apply what you have just learned about how to "take captive every thought to make it obedient to Christ," beginning with those thoughts that most frequently disturb you. When these thoughts come, take the advice of the masters and drop them at once, returning your attention to the present moment. Write your plan here but remember, it may need to be amended as you continue to learn your way to peace of soul.

_____

_____

_____

_____

_____

_____

_____

_____

_____

_____

_____

5. Use this space to record your progress.

_____

_____

_____

_____

_____

_____

_____

_____

CHAPTER THREE

THE PRACTICE
OF THE
PRESENCE OF GOD

Thus far we have learned how important it is to calm our minds so that we can remain focused on the present moment where God reveals His will for our lives. But God does a lot more than just reveal His will for us in the present moment – He reveals *Himself* to us.

As Jesus told the mystic, Blessed Conchita de Armida "I want to close the distances that separate Me from souls; I want them to know Me as I am: Not Jesus who lived in the past, but a present Jesus, not only in the tabernacle, but also in the intimacy of each heart."[54]

He not only wants to direct us in every moment of our lives, He wants to share every moment of our lives with us and to do so personally. In other words, he wants to live your life with *you*, not with your spouse or your children or your siblings or your friends – with *you*.

---

54 De Armida, Conchita, *To My Priests*, 1929 pg. 114

This is what Jesus meant when He told us: "Whoever loves me will keep my word, and my Father will love Him and we will come to him and make our dwelling with him."[55]

The question we need to ask ourselves at this juncture is a simple one – what am I doing with this greatest of all gifts?

Many of us bemoan the absence of worshipers before the tabernacle in our churches, but an even worse offense is how many of the baptized leave Our Lord in lonely abandonment within the tabernacles of their own souls. Even the pious frequently overlook this precious treasure Who waits so patiently for a nod of recognition from us.

We may think that awareness of God is something that belongs within the confine of a Church, or during a prescribed prayer time, but this is not true. He wants this awareness from all of us, all of the time, but we too often settle for much less than He wants to give us.

"God has infinite treasures to give us, yet we are satisfied with a bit of perceptible devotion that passes in an instant."[56]

For those who discover this precious treasure, however, life is never the same again.

How could this be? When one becomes continually aware of the Presence within them Who is the Creator of Universes, the Architect of Time, the Lord of Life, and the great I Am, it changes *everything*.

In a way, it's almost terrifying to think that such greatness can inhabit us by baptismal grace, but when we come to grips with this reality and really begin to live it, we

---

55 John 14:23
56 Brother Lawrence of the Resurrection, *The Practice of the Presence of God, Critical Edition* (Washington, DC; *ICS Publications,* 1994-2015) pg 54

can never be the same person again.

This is the coveted prize awarded to the soul who is willing to love God and trust Him enough to live in the present moment - the gift of Himself and all the graces we need to live in that present moment. Of all the reasons to remain focused on the present moment, this is surely the most compelling of all.

Acquiring the habit of living in constant awareness of the indwelling God is known as the Practice of the Presence of God. Although many souls lived it through the ages, it was coined with this name in the writings of Brother Lawrence of the Resurrection, a Discalced Carmelite brother who lived at a monastery in Paris during the 17th century.

He was a simple man who considered himself to be clumsy and inept and deserving of no higher work than repairing broken sandals or making soup in the kitchen of the monastery.

Yet it was to this humble man, in the nondescript moments of drudgery while sweating over the fire in a kitchen or in a damp and dimly lit workshop, that God revealed the secrets of His Kingdom here on earth. These secrets were revealed to us in a small collection of letters written three hundred years ago which became one of the Church's most beloved classics, *The Practice of the Presence of God*.

As Brother Lawrence taught. "He is always near you and with you; do not leave him alone. You would consider it rude to leave a friend who is visiting you by himself; then why abandon God and leave him alone. Do not forget Him. Think of Him often, adore him continually, live and die with Him. This is the true occupation of a Christian; in a word, this is our trade. If we don't know it, we must learn it!"[57]

---

[57] *The Practice of the Presence of God*, pg. 75

He calls it "the holiest and most necessary practice in the spiritual life" that is nothing more than "an application of our mind to God, or a remembrance of God present, that can be brought about by either the imagination or the understanding."[58]

Of course, this doesn't mean that we spend our whole day paying attention to God and nothing else because that would be impossible. Rather, he describes this as a "simple attentiveness and a general loving awareness of God" that is more like a quiet and secret conversation of the soul with God.

St. Teresa of Avila used an analogy to describe this kind of awareness. She compares the soul to a person "who is with others in a very bright room; and then suppose that the shutters are closed so that the people are all in darkness. The light by which they can be seen has been taken away, and, until it comes back, we shall be unable to see them, yet we are none the less aware that they are there."[59]

It's a subtle, unobtrusive kind of awareness that is always there even though we are not always focused on it; somewhat like the background music playing in a hotel lobby. We only hear it when we tune into it.

This tuning in can be accomplished in a variety of ways ranging from a quick glance within to pay attention for a moment to His presence within, to a prayer or other act of adoration sandwiched between running household errands, business meetings or classes.

"God does not ask a great deal of us; a brief remembrance from time to time, a brief act of adoration, occasionally to ask Him for His grace or offer Him your

---

58 Ibid, pg. 42
59 Teresa of Avila, *The Interior Castle*, Translated and Edited by E. Allison Peers, (New York, NY; *Image Books Doubleday*, 1989) pg. 211

sufferings, at other times to thank Him for the graces He has given you and is giving you."[60]

Regardless of how we choose to recognize the Presence of God within us, we should not hesitate to "find consolation in him as often as possible," Brother Lawrence recommends. "During your meals and conversations, occasionally lift up your heart to him; the least little remembrance of him will always be most agreeable."[61]

In his case, these remembrances were more than just agreeable. Brother Lawrence frequently told his friends that God let nothing go by without immediately rewarding him a hundredfold, often giving him such great experiences and glimpses of His divinity that these sometimes overwhelmed him.

"It's too much, Lord, it's too much for me!" he would sometimes protest.

"I cannot understand how a soul who is with God, and wants Him alone, is capable of suffering," he once remarked. Even though he felt deserving of nothing but suffering, he would experience "such continual profound joys that I have trouble keeping them under control."[62]

This is why he once remarked that he felt as if the Lord had deceived Him by promising the cross and yet giving him so much joy.

Of course he suffered in life, as we all do, but this suffering was very much mitigated by his constant awareness of the presence of Eternal Joy.

60 *The Practice of the Presence of God*, pg. 73
61 Ibid
62 Ibid

As this practice continued to develop in him, Brother Lawrence said, "I began to live as if only He and I existed in the world."[63]

In essence, this is the way it will become for all of us who live in the presence of God because the place He inhabits is that of our very soul, which is the core of who we are, the "who" that no one but ourselves and God knows.

As time goes on, out of such an intimate relationship as this, we naturally being to develop a real dependence on God in all of the events of life, just as Brother Lawrence did.

For example, when faced with the struggles to develop himself in a particular virtue, he would call out, "My God, I can only do this if you help me,"[64] and he would immediately receive all the strength he needed, plus some.

When he failed at something, he would acknowledge his mistake and tell God, "I will never do anything right if you leave me alone; it's up to you to stop me from failing and correct what is wrong."[65] Once said, he would go back to his business and no longer worry about his failure.

For this reason, Brother Lawrence advised souls to act very straightforwardly with God, and speak to Him freely, asking Him for help in events as they happen, for God never fails to come to our aid, as he often experienced.[66]

As Brother Lawrence proved, there is no better way to approach God than through the ordinary workings of everyday life. We don't need to seclude ourselves in monasteries, perform austere penances, or spend extraordinary amounts of time in prayer. Instead, "we must

---

63 Ibid
64 Ibid, pg. 100
65 Ibid
66 Ibid

be just as closely united with God during our activities as we are during our times of prayer."[67]

However, this doesn't mean that we give up prayer time and fall into the trap of thinking that "our work is our prayer." Consistent and devoted prayer time remains the gold standard for spiritual progress. But at the same time, this devoted time for prayer shouldn't be our only recourse to God during the day. He is with us 24 hours a day, seven days a week, and wants nothing more than for us to begin to enjoy that astonishing reality.

So how do we do this? Where do we begin to teach ourselves how to practice the Presence of God?

To start, let us first look at what it means to be present to someone.

According to Father John Hardon, "presence" always describes a relationship between people. A desk can't be present to us, but a person can be.

"When ... we imply that two or more people are somehow present to one another, it makes a big difference whom we are speaking of as being present to whom, whether it's A present to B, or B present to A, because A can be present to B and B might not be present to A," Father Hardon explains.[68]

In other words, we can be sitting right next to someone and not be in the least bit present to them because our attention is elsewhere.

This leads us to the all important question. "Is it true that we are always present to God?"

---

67 Ibid, pg. 107
68 Hardon, Father John SJ, "Living in the Presence of God," accessed online at The Real Presence Association

"Yes," Father Hardon writes. "God must sustain us, so surely we must be present to Him. Is it also true that God is always present to us, physically, as the omnipresent divine reality? Yes. He is always present to us by His infinity or, as I prefer to say, physically, because the reality of God is always affecting or influencing us.

"Admitting that God is always present to us physically, is He always present to us spiritually? No, no more than a person who is physically next to us in a room is present to us spiritually unless or until we somehow respond to his or her being there. A person may be physically present in a room, but unless we are somehow aware of that person being there, and respond to that presence, he or she might just as well not be there."[69]

It is this spiritual presence of God that we want to acquire.

And it is achieved simply by willing it.

"If we wish to cultivate living in the presence of God, we must first make the decision to think about God . . . We must see Him with that strange power we have of recalling people we want to think about," Father Hardon instructs.[70]

This echoes the words of Brother Lawrence himself who wrote, "We cannot be with Him unless we think of Him often."[71]

Remember, even though we may not be able to be there physically for someone, spiritually we're not confined to space and time which means spirit can be present to spirit, Father writes.

---

69 Ibid
70 "Living in the Presence of God"
71 *Practice of the Presence of God*, pg. 72

For instance, a person may be in Philadelphia and another in Chicago but they can both think about and therefore be spiritually present to one another.

"Or the one present to us may be long since dead – dead in body, not spirit. Centuries may separate us from that person. No matter. By that mysterious alchemy of the spirit, the moment we begin thinking of him or her – but we have to begin by thinking – they become literally present to us."[72]

This is why it's so important to create similar opportunities during the day to be "thought-full" of God, Father Hardon writes.

"If we wish to foster living in God's presence, we must make sure that He first comes to our attention outside of the mind in order that He will enter inside the mind . . ."[73]

For this reason, Father Hardon recommends that we keep sacred objects and images of God in our homes to continually remind us of Him.

However, thinking about Him is just the start. "Clearly, just thinking about God is not yet living in God's presence in the way in which we know we should as Christians," Father Hardon writes. "God must also, and especially, be in our wills. Here we have Christ's own formula for cultivating this presence of God. At the Last Supper, among other things, He said, 'If anyone loves me he will keep my word,' meaning: he will do my will, 'and my Father will love him, and we shall come to him and make our home with him.' The 'if' is up to us - always, of course, with God's grace; the 'and', in this case, is up to God. We take care of the 'if' and He will take care of the 'and'."[74]

---

72 "Living in the Presence of God"
73 Ibid
74 "Living in the Presence of God"

This passage outlines the perfect method for living in God's presence with our wills. "It means simply and unequivocally that we try as far as possible always to say 'yes' to God's will in our lives."[75]

This "yes" must be said to all that occurs in every moment of every day.

Yes, it's difficult, but not when we consider the prize – the peace and joy that comes from living in the present moment, in the Presence of God.

Brother Lawrence gives us several important rules for learning how to live in the Presence of God.

First, it requires great purity of life, meaning that we actively seek Christian perfection through the avoidance of sin, the practice of the virtues, and regular participation in prayer and the Sacraments.

Second, we must have great fidelity to the practice of this Presence and the fostering of this awareness of God. However this "must always be performed gently, humbly, and lovingly, without giving into disturbance or anxiety."[76]

Third, we must get into the habit of recalling this Presence, regardless of how briefly, before undertaking our duties, and then renewing this recollection from time to time. For example, first thing in the morning ask the Lord to grant you the great grace of being present to Him throughout the day. Then, as the day progresses, renew the request either with words or just an inward glance.

Fourth, create your own brief ejaculations that can be used to recall the Presence of the Lord, being careful to

---

75 Ibid
76 *The Practice of the Presence of God*, pg. 4e

form them from the heart. Don't be afraid to get personal with Him! "Be with me, Lord!" or even just a simple, "Hello, Lord!"

" . . . [T]his presence of God must be maintained more by the heart and by love than by the understanding or by discourse. In the ways of God, thoughts amount to little whereas love counts for everything."[77]

This makes as much sense naturally as it does spiritually. Isn't it love that fuels us to keep in touch with those we love? How often during the day do we "check in" with our spouse or children? It should be the same way with God. We should also "check in" with Him in whatever way the heart moves us to do. Make up your own "sweet little nothings" that can flow between your heart and His during the course of the day. It can be something as simple as a "thinking of you!" or "love you, Lord!" in between classes, a pause in a business meeting, or folding laundry. This is what makes the practice of the presence of God so special – it's unique to each one of us.

We must beware of letting discouragement stop us from making the effort to practice the presence of God.

"Since much time and effort are required to acquire this practice, we must not get discouraged when we fail, for the habit is only formed with effort, yet once it is formed we will find contentment in everything."[78]

---

77 *The Practice of the Presence of God*, pg. 126
78 Ibid, pg. 44

Practicum

1. In the previous chapter, you embarked upon the challenge of taking control of destructive thought patterns by dropping these thoughts immediately and returning to the present moment. Now it's time to not only return to the present moment, but to the God Who lives in your present moments. Before this becomes a habit of the heart, start by establishing set times during the day when you will stop what you're doing and "be present" to the God within – just before lunch break, driving home in the car, cooking dinner, watching television (commercials are a great time to "check in" with the Lord!). Try to set three times during the day for this practice – morning, noon, and night – or whatever natural breaks occur in your daily life. Jot down your plan here and record your progress over the next few days. Make adjustments where necessary.

_____

_____

_____

_____

_____

_____

_____

_____

_____

_____

2. Remember, this part of the practice takes effort. It won't be easy, and it could take a long time before it becomes habitual. You might be completely focused one day, and the next you barely gave it a thought. God understands the human condition and is just waiting for you to say those two words that have

made saints out of so many sinners – "help me!" Make a list of everything that seems to be preventing you from focusing on God in the moment – whether it be worries about past problems, a future event, overwhelming pressures in the present, or just plain inattention. Next to each one, write down that short and most effective prayer–"help me!"

_____

_____

_____

_____

_____

_____

_____

_____

_____

_____

3. It's very easy to get discouraged when we're trying to acquire a new discipline. Pray often to the Holy Spirit for the gift of fortitude that He will help you to persevere.

Come, O Blessed Spirit of Fortitude,
uphold my soul in time of trouble and adversity,
sustain my efforts after holiness,
strengthen my weakness,
give me courage against all the
assaults of my enemies,
that I may never be overcome and
separated from Thee,
my God and greatest Good.
Amen.[1]

---

1 Accessed on the EWTN website at https://www.ewtn.com/devotion-als/pentecost/seven_tx.htm

CHAPTER FOUR

ABANDONMENT – THE KEY TO SUCCESS

Now that you have been introduced to the Catholic version of mindfulness, and have been given the time to assess exactly what challenges lie ahead for you in implementing this new and more mindful way of life, it's time to reveal the secret to success.

It can be summed up in one word – *abandonment.*

The time has come for you to learn, once and for all, that if you want to get anywhere in this practice – or any other spiritual endeavor – you must stop trying to do it yourself and put all your trust in God.

The time has come to learn the reality of what the spiritual masters call "the two great props" of the spiritual life:

1) Trust in God
2) Distrust in Self

These two "great props" always go together. We can't have one without the other. For example, we're not trusting in God when we're really trusting in ourselves and our own initiative in the spiritual life. Neither can we achieve this essential distrust of self without trusting in God because then we would have no reliable support. It would be like embarking upon a journey with no compass and, therefore, no surety of ever reaching our destination.

This vital lesson is the essence of the Little Way of Spiritual Childhood as taught by St. Therese of Lisieux:

"Spiritual childhood is the way of confidence and abandonment . . . It means that we acknowledge our nothingness; that we expect everything from the good Lord, as a child expects everything from its father; it means to worry about nothing . . . It also means not to attribute to ourselves the virtues we practice, not to believe we are capable of anything, but to acknowledge that it is the good Lord who has placed that treasure in the hand of His little child that He may use it when He needs it, but it remains always God's own treasure."[79]

Absolute and unequivocal surrender to the Lord is the essence of humility. It is acquired only when we come to a full realization of who we are – and who we are not.

As de Caussade reminds, "Everything good in you originates in God; everything evil, spoilt, and corrupt originates in yourself. Set aside then, nothingness and sin, evil habits and inclinations, abysmal weakness and wretchedness. These are your portion; these originate in, and unquestionably belong to, you. Everything else – the body and its senses, the soul and its energies, the modicum of good you have performed – are God's portion. It so

---

[79] St. Therese of Lisieux: *Her Last Conversations*, translated by John Clarke, OCD (Washington, DC: *ICS Publications*, 1977) pg. 138

manifestly belongs to him that you realize you cannot claim one whit of it as yours, nor feel one grain of complacency, without being guilty of theft and larceny against God."[80]

Make no mistake, this truth about ourselves is a cold, hard reality – and a terrifying one for those who have no faith or trust in God. But we who do have faith have no need to "fear the terrors of the night"[81] because, as St. Therese teaches, we know that we have a good and loving God who delights in helping His children achieve sanctity.

Even though we all know this to be true, why do so few of us live that way? What makes it so difficult for us weak and pathetic creatures, in need of even the most basic assistance in the spiritual life, to turn to the One Who has all that we need? Why are we so insistent upon doing things ourselves?

There are many reasons why an individual might find it difficult to abandon himself to his Creator, but one of the most common is our fear of loss.

"Abandonment inevitably requires an element of renunciation and it is this that is most difficult for us. We have a natural tendency to cling to a whole host of things: material goods, affections, desires, projects, etc. and it costs us terribly to let go of our grip, because we have the impression that we will lose ourselves in the process, that we will die," explains Father Jacques Philippe.[82]

For this reason, we have a tendency to divide our existence into various sectors, giving certain sectors over to God with confidence, but withholding others to be managed

80 De Caussade, Father J.P., *Self Abandonment to Divine Providence* (Rockford, IL; *Tan Books and Publishers, Inc.,* 1987) pg 196
81 Psalm 91:5
82 Philippe, Father Jacques, *Searching for and Maintaining Peace* (Staten Island, NY: *St. Paul,* 2002) pg. 37

by ourselves. In other words, we may trust Him with our prayer life, but not our retirement fund.

As a result, we don't give Him *carte blanche,* which is what He wants. Instead, we keep some areas to ourselves, and these areas become the source of the same fear and anxiety that we're trying to escape. By holding back, we only perpetuate our own feelings of uneasiness.

"The measure of our interior peace will be that of our abandonment, consequently of our detachment," Father Philippe writes.[83]

However, if we give God what He wants, which is *everything,* we discover a truth that the devil works very hard to hide from us – that God asks for everything, but He doesn't necessarily *take* everything.

"Faced with certain goods that we possess (a material good, a friendship, an activity that we enjoy, etc.), the devil, in an effort to prevent us from abandoning ourselves to God, causes us to imagine that if we put everything in God's hands, God will effectively take everything and 'ruin' everything in our lives! And this arouses a sense of terror that completely paralyzes us."[84]

However, as Father explains, we need not fall into this trap!

"Very frequently . . . the Lord asks only an attitude of detachment at the level of the heart, a disposition to give Him everything. But He doesn't necessarily 'take' everything. He leaves us in peaceful possession of many things when they are not bad in themselves and can serve His designs."[85]

---

83 *Searching for and Maintaining Peace,* pg. 37
84 Ibid, pg. 39
85 Ibid

For those times when He does require effective detachment, He will enable us to clearly understand the reason in good time, Father says.

"He will give us the necessary strength. And this detachment, even though it is painful at the moment, will be followed by profound peace. The proper attitude then is to be disposed to give everything to God, without panic, and to allow Him to do things His way, in total confidence."[86]

Another temptation is to convince ourselves that there is something about our situation that just makes it impossible to give ourselves totally to God. For instance, we might be in the midst of a difficult time financially, pressured by demands of family, or don't have the gifts and qualities that are needed by someone who wants to achieve this level of Christian perfection.

"We often live with this illusion," writes Father Philippe. "But this is often an error. It is not the exterior circumstances that must change; it is above all our hearts that must change. They must be purified of their withdrawal into themselves, of their sadness, of their lack of hope."[87]

Regardless of our circumstances, God is present, and it is well within His power to provide for whatever we need to acquire sanctity.

In fact, often the very circumstances we think are so negative and damaging to our ability to abandon ourselves to God's will are actually God's pedagogy and, therefore, the most powerful means at our disposal to progress and grow.

For example, our fear of losing our job can teach us how useless it is to trust only in those who employ us. While we humans naturally need to feel security to thrive,

---

86 Ibid
87 Ibid, pg. 42-43

learning how to find our security in God alone teaches us how to acquire a sense of being safe that can transcend what happens on the natural level and make us stronger and more confident individuals. Eventually, we will be able to say, "As long as I'm with God, I'll be okay." Imagine how much less fear would sneak into our lives if we learned just this one vital lesson!

Another reason that prevents us from abandoning ourselves to God, perhaps the most common of all, is that we're too busy worrying to be able to "let go and let God." Some of us believe that if we worry enough it won't happen – which is superstition. We can attend to our circumstances without giving in to anxiety.

As Father Jean du Coeur de Jesus D'Elbee warns, we must never consent consciously to anxiety or a troubled mind because then we are acting like the apostles did while sailing across the lake of Tiberias. There was Jesus, sleeping in the boat beside them, and yet they became terrified when the sea turned turbulent.

As Father Jean writes, he can almost hear Jesus scolding the apostles – and us – with gentleness but also with a little pain as well.

"I was in the boat with you – I slept, but I was there – and you were afraid, you were terrified. You doubted either my omnipotence or my love. Do you not know after all who I am, and do you not know after all with what tenderness my Heart watches over you continually?"[88]

Nothing offends Jesus more than when we worry voluntarily, Father writes. This wounds His heart like nothing else because it means we don't trust Him.

---

88 Pere Jean du Coeur de Jesus D'Elbee, *I Believe in Love* (Petersham, MA; *St. Bede's Publications*, 1972) pg. 24

This kind of voluntary worry means that we are worrying with the full consent of the will.

There is a big difference between our human nature and our will. Human nature feels worry and anxiety - but the will is what enables us to consent to it.

As Father Jean teaches, "My nature says 'no' but my will says 'yes'. My nature trembles; with all my will, I smile through my tears. My nature is troubled and afraid; my nature revolts, I force myself to say, 'All is well, Jesus, do not change anything'."[89]

Even if we have to make a prayer out of the words for which Jesus reproached His apostles, "Lord, save us, we are perishing!" so be it. Anything is better than deliberately worrying – which is with the full consent of the will -because as long as we do so, we will be depriving ourselves of achieving the loving trust and abandonment to God that we seek.

But what if, for one reason or another, we just can't bring ourselves to take that step of abandonment to God? What then?

Do it anyway, the masters tell us, even if just in the form of mere words at first. "Jesus, I surrender this to you." If you don't have the desire to even do this much, ask God to give you the desire to desire to do it.

Always remember that "Abandonment is not natural; it is a grace to be asked of God. He will give it to us if we pray with perseverance."[90]

So if you're relying on yourself to accomplish this, you might as well stop right here. Do not take another step

---

89 Ibid
90 Ibid

forward without asking God to do for you what you are unable to do for yourself.

The grace of abandonment will come soon enough!

While we're waiting, however, we can make good use of the time by properly preparing ourselves to receive this gift of abandonment by asking the Holy Spirit to strengthen us in the virtue of hope.

This frequently misunderstood virtue is not about hoping everything will turn out the way we want. As Father Gabriel of St. Mary Magdalen explains, for the person of faith, hope is what reassures us that regardless of what may happen to us in this life, we have a great and awesome God who belongs to us and who we can count on to fulfill His promises to us.

"We look at the infinite God who is perfect and immensely higher than our self, a weak, miserable creature, and we wonder: How can I ever reach Him and be united with Him who is so infinitely beyond my capacity? And hope replies: You can, for God Himself wishes it. . ."[91]

All believers must have a firm hope in the help of God which He repeatedly promises in Scripture to those who love Him.

"Ask and it shall be given you."[92]

"My God will fully supply whatever you need, in accord with his glorious riches in Christ Jesus."[93]

---

91 Father Gabriel of St. Mary Magdalen, OCD, *Divine Intimacy* (Rockford, IL; *Tan Books and Publishers*, 1996) pg. 735.
92 Matthew 7:7
93 Philippians 4:19

"If God so clothes the grass of the field, which grows today and is thrown into the oven tomorrow, will he not much more provide for you, O you of little faith?"[94]

"If God is for us, who can be against us? He who did not spare his own Son but handed him over for us all, how will he not also give us everything else along with him?"[95]

As Father Gabriel reminds us, it would be rash to hope that God will save and sanctify us without our cooperation, but if we sincerely strive to avoid faults and to practice virtue generously, "we can hope with certainty that He will do for us what we, in spite of all our efforts, can never succeed in doing. God wants us to be certain of this."[96]

With much prayer and cooperation on our part, this certainty develops over time, and, as it develops, so does our confidence in God. This confidence will ultimately enable us to trust our great God who asks for – and so richly deserves – our complete and total abandonment.

Consider the development of this process in the great saint, St. Margaret Mary, who often heard the Lord say to her during life, "Let me do it." But it wasn't until her death that she finally realized what he was trying to tell her.

"His Sacred Heart will do everything for me if I let him. He shall will, he shall love, he shall desire for me and make up for my faults."[97]

The question we must all ask ourselves is this – will you let Him?

---

94 Matthew 6:30
95 Romans 8:31-32
96 *Divine Intimacy*, pg 735
97 Pere Jean du Coeur de Jesus D'Elbee, *I Believe in Love*, (Petersham, MA; *St. Bede's Publications*, 1974), pg. 51

How many times a day does Jesus say to us, "Let me do it" while we stand there wringing our hands over a child

who left the church, our finances, our jobs, the housework, our relationships, and a myriad of other daily concerns.

Buried beneath the cacophony of our fretful anxiety, Jesus whispers, "Let me do it."

"Like St. Margaret Mary, you may hear Jesus a hundred times a day, saying to you, 'Let me do it.' In your difficulties, in your problems, in all those things in your daily life which are sometimes so difficult, so distressing, when you ask yourself, 'What shall I do? How shall I do it?' listen to Him saying to you, 'Let me do it.' And then answer Him, 'O Jesus, I thank you for all things.' And it will be the most beautiful dialogue of love between a soul and the all-powerful and all-loving God!"[98]

However, in order to acquire the kind of hope that allows us to live in such utter abandonment to God, there is one other virtue that we need to develop within ourselves – the virtue of generosity.

"Generosity is the virtue which teaches us to spend ourselves, without counting the cost, without ever saying, 'It is enough;' it teaches us to give ourselves completely, and to work with the maximum of love, not only in great things, but also in little ones, even the least."[99]

This virtue will gradually help us conquer our inherent selfishness and enable us to give ourselves totally without being hampered by personal preoccupations.

"Selfishness, preoccupation with self, and

98 Ibid, pg. 52
99 *Divine Intimacy*, pg. 868

discouragement, are all enemies of generosity; they are 'earth and lead' which weigh down our spiritual life, making it more fatiguing and keeping us from soaring to the heights."[100]

Gradually, as we turn our focus away from ourselves and toward God, who is orchestrating all the moments of our life, we naturally begin to learn how to forget ourselves, our own interests, our convenience. These begin to dwindle in importance as God's interests slowly become our interests.

This is a gradual process that can take a lifetime. As St. Francis de Sales once said, "You do not put on perfection the way you put on a dress."[101]

We must also be careful not to presume that we can acquire this generous abandonment faster by sinking into a kind of quietism, a heresy which denies the necessity of human activity in the pursuit of sanctification. Instead of actively worshiping our God in prayer and works, quietism turns inward into a kind of passive stillness.

"Perfect abandonment differs from quietism because it is accompanied by hope and unwavering fidelity to duty, even in little things, from moment to moment . . ."[102]

We must always do our part, fumbling and inept as it might be; and never forget what we learned earlier in this chapter - that every good effort and the goodwill from which it stems, comes from Him.

It's also important to note that achieving this level of abandonment doesn't mean that we'll never worry or suffer any anxiety. Of course we will, because this is part of the

---

100 Ibid
101 Quoted in *Self-Abandonment to Divine Providence*, pg. 196
102 Garrigou-Lagrange, Father Reginald, OP *The Three Ages of the Interior Life, Volume Two* (Rockford, IL:, *Tan Books and Publishers*, 1989) pg. 460

human condition. What it does mean, however, is that we won't be voluntarily or deliberately disturbed. As we learned thus far in this study, we must never consciously consent to anxiety or a troubled mind.

Instead, when we feel anxiety coming on, we must make an act of confidence such as this one, "Jesus, you are here; nothing happens, not a hair falls from my head without your permission. I have no right to worry."

What hope! What confidence! This combination, when founded upon faith, is all powerful.

"A man of faith is not one who believes that God can do everything but one who believes he can obtain everything from God."[103]

These words echo those of St. John of the Cross who so famously said, "We obtain from God as much as we hope for from him."[104]

How much do we hope for? Does our weakness, our faults, our sins, make us afraid to ask for too much? Does our unworthiness make us afraid to lift our eyes to heaven and ask for what we truly want – to live in peaceful abandonment to the will of God as it manifests itself in all of the moments of our day while basking in the Presence of Eternal Joy?

Let us cast off this discouragement by realizing what it truly is – a temptation from the devil. If we succumb, this can develop into a kind of secret despair which only the virtue of hope can remedy.

---

103 Philippe, Father Jacques, *Interior Freedom* (New York, NY: *Scepter*, 2007) pg. 107
104 St. John of the Cross, *The Collected Words of St. John of the Cross, The Dark Night* (Washington, DC; *ICS Publications*, 1991) Book Two, Chapter 10

"For the will to be strong and enterprising, it needs to be animated by desire. Desire can only be strong if what is desired is perceived as accessible, possible. We cannot effectively want something if we have the sense that 'we'll never make it'."[105]

Humans are not motivated by what we believe will end in failure. We must believe that success is possible or we will have no desire to even try.

This is why any thoughts that cause us to doubt God's desire to enable us to achieve true holiness, and the subsequent peace that it affords the believer, should be discarded immediately and replaced with one of the most powerful professions of faith and hope in the Bible: "I can do all things in Him Who strengthens me."[106]

As Father de Caussade says, "An army animated by such views would be invincible."[107]

We, too, can be invincible if we agree to the challenge God sets before us to find Him in each and every moment of our lives in order to discover in that trusting abandonment the peace that the world cannot give.

Now that we've arrived at the end of our study, it should be obvious that there is no comparison between the Catholic version of mindfulness and its Buddhist alternative.

"Compared to the broad reach of the practice of the presence of God, mindfulness is nothing more than what it is - a sterile mental exercise that focuses on a single dimension of life – that which concerns only the self.

---

105 *Interior Freedom*, pg 105-106
106 Philippians 4:13
107 *Self-Abandonment to Divine Providence*, pg. 47

There is no reciprocal awareness or loving or sharing with Another. It is empty of all but ourselves."[108]

Some claim to practice the Buddhist version of mindfulness as a way to "center" themselves before turning their focus to God, but this raises the question - why bother?

"If we're going to exert all that effort on focusing – and mindfulness does require a great deal of effort – why waste time and energy focusing on a superfluous 'side trip' when we could just skip that and invest our energy on going straight to God? Even though it's true that both practices require effort, one practice is fueled by Divine grace while the other is fueled by our own weak human efforts. Which one is more likely to succeed?"[109]

Once we allow ourselves to come to a practical understanding of the Catholic alternative to mindfulness - that God is really present within each of us at every moment of every day - feeling, thinking, hearing, seeing everything right along with us - and we become *aware* of this Presence within ourselves - a whole new dimension of life is revealed.

We suddenly become more conscious of living not only as a physical being, but also as a spiritual being. Living with God in this way becomes the ultimate form of existence, the optimal lifestyle. Nothing can surpass it because His Presence is pure joy, even during the worst moments, the most severe trials, and this Presence quickly becomes the greatest treasure of our life. In fact, we can become so intimately associated with Him that we no longer feel like ourselves without Him.

---

108 Brinkmann, Susan OCDS, *A Catholic Guide to Mindfulness* (Bessemer, AL: Avila Institute for Spiritual Direction, 2017) pg. 104
109 *A Catholic Guide to Mindfulness*, pg. 98-99.

Let us pray:

Lord, you have opened our eyes to a whole new way of living.

Please give us the grace to continue the work you started in this study.

Let us resist the temptation to become discouraged when it becomes difficult, to be hard on ourselves when we fail, to forget that you come to us in a new way in every moment of every day.

Give us the grace to pick ourselves up and start anew, no matter how many times we do so, confident that every setback is an invitation to learn something new and every failure is another opportunity to experience your mercy.

Take captive our thoughts, O Lord, so that we may give you the glory and praise that you so richly deserve. We ask all this in your holy name.

Amen.

About the Catholic Life Institute

The Catholic Life Institute, acting under the patronage of the Immaculate Heart of Mary and Our Lady of Mount Carmel, is a lay-run apostolate devoted to infusing the world with the truth and splendor of the Catholic mystical tradition as revealed by the Carmelite saints and Doctors of the Church.

The Institute was founded by members of the Immaculate Heart of Mary Chapter of Discalced Secular Carmelites from Willow Grove, Pennsylvania to introduce Carmelite spirituality and authentic Catholic contemplation to the faithful. Our programs include courses on Teresian prayer, the interior life, the Little Way of Spiritual Childhood as taught by St. Therese of Lisieux, and spiritual warfare.

Our programs are presented by Susan Brinkmann, OCDS, an award-winning Catholic journalist who serves as the Director of Communications and New Age research for Women of Grace. She is the author of several books and is a frequent guest on EWTN. Her areas of expertise are in Carmelite prayer and spirituality, the New Age, and the occult.

The Catholic Life Institute Press is our newest addition and is used to publish our workbooks and other publications. In addition to our own books, the Institute also provides a wide collection of Church-approved Catholic books at discounted prices.

Our courses, books, retreats, and seminars are faithful to the Magisterium and completely free of New Age components.

Visit us online at www.CatholicLifeInstitute.org for more information.

Made in the USA
Columbia, SC
04 August 2021

42987267R00048